SHARON ROSE

GW00993223

PIRATE TOMMY

From Toby's KS1 & KS2 Stuff 2

Part II Poems & Short Stories
By Sharon Rose

Illustrator Richard Uff

PIRATE TOMMY

DEDICATION

In His service, the Prince of Peace. For the
inspiration of His Children everywhere. Jesus loves
you.

Table of Contents

SHARON ROSE

ACKNOWLEDGEMENT

With much gratitude to our Heavenly Father for life and the gift of creativity. As He is, so are we. Thanking Toby for allowing me free rein over his initial story. I appreciate this and would forever be grateful for the gift of having children – it was all in preparation for writing for a younger audience.

I also wish to thank Richard Uff for successfully making piracy look glamorous. I could not change the storyline but it does lead to an appropriate deserving end to accommodate his finer drawings.

To readers who provided valuable feedback, I hope this meets your satisfaction. I appreciate your continued support. Thanking all initial purchasers. Please do not hesitate to present your original copy and claim your 50% discount from me. To all those contributors, suggesting font sizes to splitting up the book, thank you so much. To all those believing in my ability to see this project through, encouraging and asking when it will be ready. Your wait is over! Many thanks also to the websites where from which I lifted the picture strawberries (Bing I think). Appreciation for the endless list of Youtube self publishing gurus and Amazon KDP for making it available for me to go to print without expertise or capital. You are a gift from God. Thank you all so much for carrying me along. God richly bless you for being a blessing.

DISCLAIMER

All errors are mine. There is room for improvement and all honest feedback would be welcome.

SHARON ROSE

HIS STORY

That sin has its recompense
Of that I am sure
But should my Saviour tarry
Or I be weary
My sins and burdens will I carry
To lay down at the foot of His cross

There to serve Him who for my sin
And shame was fraught
To leave me cleansed and forgiven
That I may sin no more

PIRATE TOMMY

For my soul He won and bought
Ransomed restored blameless forevermore

His life He willingly gave
With a crown of thorns
By His precious blood shed
For my lasting victory
Deity without taint or doubt
Bearing pain just for me to draw nigh

There is no bridge that I can't cross
In the beauty of His holiness
The grave could not hold Him
When nailed to the cross
On the third day
He arose

All proclaim His goodness
Great love though foretold
He has no match in power
His love so wonderful I live to glorify
And must testify
Of healing by one Word or touch

Like the star telling of His birth
I shine brighter and brighter
To show and tell of His love
About abundant life found in Him
And let the world know that this story of old
Will always from my lip and heart unfold

PIRATE TOMMY

CHAPTER 1

PIRATE TOMMY & HIS TREASURE

A long, long, long time ago, there lived a pirate called Pirate Tommy. He was tall, wore a black hat with the usual white skeleton in the middle of his cap. You've guessed it! It was a skull and bones scary cap. He had fierce scars and many marks on his big round tummy. As a lawless Seaman, he could not avoid getting into many fights. Or being bitten by all sorts on his journeys.

I think that's why he was called Tommy. With scars that looked like a tatoo on his belly, everyone knew that he liked showing off his scars. It was as if to say 'don't even think about it, I survived worse and have scars to prove it!' He had lived for so long on the seas, he forgot his real name. Being lawless, this made him quite proud. His crew always dreaded him getting drunk because it was always the same stupid game. He would ask them to guess his real name and toss them into the sea for a swim whether freezing or shark infested waters! They have sailed for 35 long years, yet no one has ever guessed it because he could not even remember what it was.

Jolly Chair

Pirate Tommy lived on a ship called the Jolly Chair. It had a square on the floor, covering a secret panel and a staircase, leading to the cellar. That was where his chum and fellow pirate, Cheery Ale slept.

Hence his name also was acquired.

So Pirate Tommy, Cheery Ale and their crew of 18 men from Lawder Country, sailed the wild and stormy seas. Even their rivals avoided them. They were fugitives because they were not only running from the law, but they did not care about breaking the law or some heads either.

Even though they were not always the ones guilty of usurping all the merchant ships. They were always suspects because they were lazy. Nor did they fish regularly. They were not lucky enough to find treasure either.

The journey to sell their wares would normally take several days under treacherous conditions. Just because they could never return to dock at Lawder Country. If they docked, it was in secret, when all the good people were sleeping in their homes. They were really that scary and had a terrible reputation. Even the Sheriff had orders to arrest them on sight! There were wanted posters everywhere for all of them, except Cheery Ale. They did not want to risk getting arrested and taken to the Tower of Dread without trial. No one wanted to be hanged! Especially, without trial. Although some people felt sorry for them because they felt that they were paying too much tax. But they were more scared of the pirates. They wanted to feel safe and everything about the pirates was shrouded in intrigue and mystery.

So they had no choice but to keep sailing around the world.

CHAPTER 2

One day, there was a heavy storm which broke and tore through Cheery Ale's favourite hammock. It left a crack on Jolly Chair too. Cheery Ale was very sad. So Pirate Tommy and the rest of the crew quickly did what they could to repair their only home. Then decided to cheer him up by going for a swim. Along they swum until they arrived at a nearby island. It looked very safe because the only scary creature that they spotted was a lizard hurtling away at the sound of their booming voices. "Oi! Ahoy!" they exclaimed. "We can build us a jolly tree house here!" one explained.

So off they went to gather rhun palm and fronds to build a cosy tree house very quickly. Mind you, this was without any permission from the landowner. They were sure that absolutely no one else, had ever set foot in those parts.

Let me explain here that the reason Pirates were not popular was because they applied the piracy law of the high seas. This was a 'finders keepers' sea tradition, even when they were on land. And that was just unacceptable to Landlords.

They then returned to Jolly Chair to fetch the rest of the crew and anchor on the island whilst the rest of the hammock was repaired.

Alas, the next day, the island was almost flooded because of a bigger storm. So they rushed aboard the ship. Which was a good idea because their tree house could not stay afloat!

Finders Keepers

Soon after, Pirate Tommy spotted something bobbing along. He quickly swam towards what looked like a treasure chest. He got closer and closer, with his eyes bulging as his heart pumped through his mouth with excitement. His "'Ahoy! Ahoy!'" could alarm even the fiercest sea creatures. As he swam faster and deeper towards it, his men wondered why he was being so reckless. After all, the storm was only just abating. Due to this however, they decided it was the wrong time to ask questions. He was already in a bad temper. So they gently hurled a rope when he beckoned and winched the chest onboard as fast as they could. Once the rope was secured around it, Pirate Tommy rushed back aboard Jolly Chair. Not wishing to be separated from his precious find. What a nightmare. As pirates they could not even trust fellow comrades on the lawless high seas. They knew about all the wicked tricks that others had experienced.

Everyone on board agreed that they had never seen Pirate Tommy swim so fast! They did not have time to plan anything. Besides, not all of the original mean crew members were still onboard. These ones since rescuing a Missionary had even

started discussing having rules and
establishing a code of honour for the high
seas. The Missionary had told them about
Christ and gave them a Bible. Even
though they always took oaths of allegiance
and camaraderie, they were still full of dirty
tricks. This lack of distrust was because
they knew that as fugitives themselves,
they could not run to the King's law
makers for protection. The King at that
time, applied equitable principles. Such as
'he who comes to the law must come with
clean hands'. Whereas, aside from Cheery
Ale, all of them were in quite serious
trouble with the law.

CHAPTER 3

"Don't store up treasures here on earth where they can erode away or may be stolen. Store them in heaven where they will never lose their value and are safe from thieves. If your profits are in heaven, your heart will be there too."

They quickly pried the chest open and emptied almost all the barrels of ale that they had remaining. They just could not believe their eyes! Never before had anyone ever found so much treasure.

In their reckless celebration and all night dance, to mark finding the enormous treasure trove, they could no longer close the chest at dawn. Their ship could be spotted from anywhere at night because its treasures lit up the night sky. They tried covering it with tarpaulin and stuffing it in empty barrels. The more they tried hiding it, the more it glowed because they were exposing more of it. They did not wish to attract attention, either from authorities policing the waters or rival Pirates. But they were running out of ideas and did not know what to do.

Now, Pirate Tommy was very very very very good at forecasting the weather. This is because he had been at sea for most of his life. He was worried now that Jolly Chair seemed to be brimming with treasure everywhere. It was no good to them if it got lost in a storm. They certainly could not spend it or enjoy it because to do that, they had to dock. Pirates were very unkind and known to violently attack fellow pirates in those waters. But now, they knew that even Lawder Country would be safe for them because they could afford to pay up all their debts and find good lawyers.

Something valuable to protect

So, although they were richer, the treasure was making Pirate Tommy and his friends quite unhappy. They now owned something of value that made them begin to value their lives and understand the rule of law.

Encumbered with sleepless nights and worry, Pirate Tommy had just forecasted another huge storm. They now had to keep watch even at night. Afraid of an ambush and afraid of losing precious cargo if their ship was to run aground, again. Whereas before, they were the source of terror to all.

Dabbling in the Diabolical

Fearing shipwreck, Pirate Tommy decided to allow his friend, Cheery Ale to disguise himself and return to land to bury the treasure at a marked location. He trusted Cheery Ale because he knew they had been friends for a very long time. They had been on several adventures too numerous to remember. But they had never cheated each other. Between them, they maintained their old-fashioned code of honour among thieves. Cheery Ale was not well known on land because his existence was like a myth. He was rumoured to be the swiftest, shrewdest and blithest of all the men on board. He actually believed that he was the wisest too. Meanwhile, Pirate Tommy, had no choice because he was notorious. He was sure that he was at risk of certain death. Therefore, the Pirates decided to swear an oath,

"To whom this chest belongs

Or for whom it longs

To divest it's true owners

Or forever deprive through bamboozling

Manipulating

And deceiving

May the open treasure

And spirits of the high seas living dead

betray the rogue."

Suddenly it thundered and they knew that their oath had been witnessed by the spirits of the seas. If anything kept them in check, it was superstition and tales of the living dead! They still had not read the Bible that the Missionary they had rescued had left for them. They had instead kept it in a safe place, knowing that it was sacred but never went near it. Otherwise, they would have prayed to God instead.

However, not all of them had chanted the oath correctly. When it came to the last verse of "betray the rogue", Cheery Ale had specifically refused to mention those words because he had conceived his own plans. Pirate Tommy had trusted his oldest friend and failed to notice him

PIRATE TOMMY

mumbling his own meaningless nonsense.

19

CHAPTER 4

Cheery Ale on a mission

Cheery Ale got himself disguised and was hauled overboard on a dingy. The men helped him winch their most valuable possession down. With strict instructions to trade only the items in the bag for food supplies, only after burying the treasure chest. Their provisions having run low after their overenthusiastic celebration, they had no other choice.

Cheery Ale paddled all the way to a land called Crabbylosbsteroyster Joy, anchored his boat, and went to the farthest part of the jungle. When he arrived at the point marked on their map, he buried a treasure chest and because he was superstitious he recanted the oath the crew had taken with

Pirate Tommy before burying it. Even though he knew he had swapped it with an empty chest.

Unknown to him, his friend Pirate Tommy had sent his Parrot, Chatblush on his trail. So Chatblush tailed Cheery Ale as he hiked a little longer, until he thought he had gone far enough inland to escape being tracked by the Ship's binnacle.

Just when he was about to bury the real treasure chest, he heard the eeriest spine-chilling growl. He felt so scared that he dropped the heavy chest and fled, never to return again. Legend has it that it was the ghosts of restless pirates who had been betrayed before. But only Chatblush and Pirate Tommy knew the secret.

Chatblush having returned to Pirate Tommy, narrated everything for the record. This was even though he had not missed most of the action because they had planned it together. When Chatblush finished and Pirate Tommy had updated his log for posterity, Pirate Tommy called his crew to a meeting. He told them that the ghosts of restless Pirates drove Cheery Ale running mad in the new found land. Which they later called Buccaneer Heaven.

PIRATE TOMMY

CHAPTER 5

"Do unto others as you would have then do unto you"

Buccaneer Heaven was a fortunate discovery because to find it you had to go deep past the jungle of Crabbylobsteroyster Joy. Buccaneer Heaven had remained undiscovered because no one had ever dared travel that far! Cheery Ale fleeing like a mad man had only run into it by chance. To date no one had dared go beyond because it is believed to be an abyss.

The men decided to vote whether to stay on the high seas or to settle at Buccaneer Heaven. Although they were all excited to learn of the new developments, some of them had strong sea blood and just felt there would be mutiny. They just found laws disagreeable and living on land had its own rules.

To avoid arguing, they were given time to think about it so that they could decide once they had arrived and seen the island.

They finally, arrived on Buccaneer Heaven, near Crabbylobsteroyster Joy. They rediscovered their partially buried treasure. Pirate Tommy and Chatblush rushed to open the treasure chest while the rest of the crew watched from afar because they were superstitious. Pirate Tommy was not affected by the oath because he knew that Cheery Ale had already recanted it and he was not betraying his comrades. So he opened the chest and divided their booty among all them. Securing the choicest without question, for himself.

Life in Buccaneer Heaven

Fifteen of the crew stayed with Pirate Tommy and lived happily ever after in Buccaneer Heaven. With equal shares, powers and rights to their new found land. Very soon, they were able to grow into their own very happy community and soon became rulers of a growing country. Some of them sold land and accumulated great wealth. Whilst others cultivated theirs and rented out property. That was when they learnt that being good law abiding property owners was not as easy as being lawless brutal pirates, terrorising property owners.

They regretted not paying taxes then, and were really sorry for all the wrong things they had done. Now that they understood why the rulers of Lawder Country introduced payment of taxes, they negotiated a truce. In exchange for trade, citizens of both territories were exempt from tax charges for a life. They also settled debts and fines. Hired good lawyers or defended themselves in Court so they could enjoy their new life and freedom to move freely.

Back to the story. After the treasure was fairly divided, 3 of the pirates decided to return to sea. So they took their share and headed back to sea to recruit their own crew. Content to have a decent friendly country to visit when they missed their friends. Some say that they never saw their friends again because Crabbylobsteroyster Joy had too many mazes leading to the abyss and no one dared risk it without a guide. Besides they no longer had access to Chatblush.. This made it such a hideaway, that few risked the dangers of trying to get there!

As for Cheery Ale, stories are still being told that he can be spotted fleeing from the growling, howling eerie voices he imagined pursuing him.

But Pirate Tommy and his friends had lots of stories to tell their grandchildren. They never experienced piracy so they were much happier. For now, they were being well trained in the ways of the of Lord so none of their children would ever return to piracy. Yet, this was only one of their many adventures so it is true that stories are still being told of pirates to this day.

PIRATE TOMMY

♫♫≈≈≈≈≈≈≈≈≈♫♫

From the Good Friday to Pirate Tommy
Wasn't he savvy?
Though this was not the treasure Jesus had
in mind
It teaches us all to be honest
And hold our words true
Because friendship is a bond
So dear
He who has ears let him hear
Cheats will be found out
When it is a wicked thing to do
Judgement day shall come to rue.

♫♫≈≈≈≈≈≈≈≈≈♫♫

TOBY'S STRAWBERRY
SUMMER

Strawberries are red
Apples are sometimes the colour of Israel's face
And I love eating soup for dinner
No baguette or bun
Crouton doesn't sound like fun

Grapes can be green
Robot drink is my invention
And mummy and Israel
I don't want to be mean
But they use the toilet

I like to keep busy eating peacefully
And enjoy eating all my fresh fish and vegetables
Except Israel and mummy
Do not eat too much
But don't be greedy

30

PIRATE TOMMY

By the end of lunchtime
When I hear the bell
I'm only ever half finished
Crunching away on crisps which I never forget
But I am not saying eat unhealthy things

Or do not eat chocolates
Nor strawberries and cream
Relax there is no rush
This is really living and there is next summer
So it does not always have to be a dream

PIRATE TOMMY

ABOUT THE AUTHOR

Sharon Rose is the Author's pseudonym. Pirate Tommy is Part II of a trilogy, written in London in 2009.

Her works are underpinned by her Christian beliefs. With lots of Biblical undertones, normally referenced as a yardstick for societal values and morals. Or a source of joy, peace, liberty, inspiration, hope, information, knowledge and even entertainment.

Pirate Tommy is part of a project created to immortalise Toby's schoolwork. This is Part II from Toby's KS1 & KS2 Stuff. Which incidentally is a miracle because they lost everything., including School photographs.

The Author now lives in Walsall with Toby. Having been on numerous 'adventures' in London, Uganda and The Gambia. Which has now inspired material for books for all age groups.

The Author has a solid legal background training, adjudicating, supporting in Secretarial capacity, proofreading, research and paralegal roles. She recently worked as a Medical Secretary, Parcel Sorter and a Warehouse Operator. Being unable to pursue further studies at BPP, she is currently a Warehouse Associate.

PIRATE TOMMY

Printed in Great Britain
by Amazon

64380083R00026